EMOTIONAL TERRORISM

EMOTIONAL
TERRORISM

Joolz

BLOODAXE BOOKS

Poems & drawings copyright © Joolz 1990

ISBN: 1 85224 136 5

First published 1990 by
Bloodaxe Books Ltd,
P.O. Box 1SN,
Newcastle upon Tyne NE99 1SN.

Bloodaxe Books Ltd acknowledges
the financial assistance of Northern Arts.

Second impression 1991

To Justin

Typesetting by EMS Phototypesetting, Berwick upon Tweed.

Printed in Great Britain by
Bell & Bain Limited, Glasgow, Scotland.

Contents

In the family

We could have kept it contained.
We could have kept it to ourselves,
with no public prying eyes
and some hope of salvation.
It would have been better.
It would have been quieter.
The knowledge of damnation,
the stench of failure...
Night after night, I could only ask why
and only hear your refusal to respond.
My own breathing whispers in my ears,
my own blood hammers in your veins.
You look at me with viper's eyes
and my tongue refuses to obey me.
Where were you? Where have you been?
Is it starting again? Is it? Is it? Is it?
More courts, more fear, more echoes of shame.
In hospital rooms the family dissected,
while you and I sit unable to command
our fate in the experts' hands.
We could have kept it contained,
we could have kept it to ourselves,
if we were not blood strangers
in a world made strange and bloody
and I can't understand,
I can't understand...

Across the threshold

When I answered the door
he was stood there, hands in his pockets,
there was no reason not to let him in,
but when he stepped across the threshold
I felt a shiver, like a warning...
something in his eyes, something alien
and unreachable, blank as a shark.
I thought it was a trick of the light,
I mean, I'd known him so long,
he's my best friend's husband, after all;
he said he'd come to see if I was all right
while Mark was away.
I made him a cup of tea,
and he watched me all the time.
I felt his eyes on me like a trap
like a net drawing tight, like a noose.
It was as if my body knew something
that my mind wouldn't accept.
In a strange way when he grabbed me
I wasn't surprised, I just went crazy
with revulsion, I screamed and fought
but he shoved me face down onto the sofa,
held my head down, I couldn't breath,
I thought I'd die, I wanted to die
while he did it to me,
battering at me, hurting me,
tearing me up while I fought to breathe
in the dust and tears...
He bit me so hard I felt his
teeth close in my skin...

Afterwards, as I lay there, he laughed at me,
he said not to tell anyone
because no one would believe me,
certainly not Sara, she'd think I was crazy,
I can't eat, you know, I can't sleep,
I can't pull myself together.
All I can feel is how he hurt me,

and how my life will never be
the same again, because of him,
with no trust, and no freedom
from it all my days...

The game

In the cheap nightclub, while the lights flash
and the music grinds, you and your friend
sit terrified, while this fat casual
yells abuse at you, the dirty words spewing
from his twisted mouth like filthy water.
You are nothing to him really,
he doesn't know you and he doesn't want to.
He just wants to frighten you and make you cry,
so you'll run to your boyfriends,
who will defend you and give him
the gang fight that he wants.
You're just the bait, the trap, the excuse,
you're the means for him to release
his vicious boredom and his rising adrenalin.

You are afraid, and fear makes you angry,
but revenge is a dish best eaten cold,
and your time will come...

Travelling alone, I lie in the white hotel room.
I am shivering, twisting the bedsheet
in my sweating hands, while the crazy man next-door
smashes up his belongings
and screams and raves all night
about how he wants to kill a woman,
any woman, if he could find one
he'd cut her, he'd rip her apart,
and only one thin wall stands between us.
I put all my clothes on quietly, and curl up,
silent tears trickling into my mouth, thinking:
if I had a gun, I'd put him down like a rabid dog...

I am afraid, and fear makes me angry,
but revenge is a dish best eaten cold,
and my time will come...

And we go about our daily lives,
all of us, woman and man, feeling in our hearts
that we have control over what happens to us;
that violence, persecution, rape happen
only to strangers that we read about
in the gutter press, until we're in the wrong place,
at the wrong time, and that cold voice
slides out of the darkness telling us
our worst fears are going to be realised,
and our spirits scream 'No, not me! Not me!
I don't deserve this!' But we are powerless,
there is no escape and our rules,
they don't matter any more, in this game...

We are afraid, and fear makes us angry,
but revenge is a dish best eaten cold,
and our time will come.

Musket, fife, and drum

'I wouldn't say he is the perfect soldier, m'Lord,
but he is a very good soldier.
Admittedly, his record isn't spotless,
but there's nothing that cannot
be accounted for by youthful high spirits
and he is very young, barely twenty,
very fit, bright, proved to be
extremely amenable to training.
There is no evidence of psychological disturbance;
however, he can give no definite explanation
or reasons for his actions. So now,
with your permission, my Lord, I should like
to call the boy to the witness box.'

'I don't know why I did it, Sir,
I think we had some stupid argument
in camp the night before
over a card game; we played cards a lot, Sir,
it's the boredom, you see,
mind you, it's enough to make anyone ratty
listening to that shelling
and those wogs killing each other
day in, day out; and nothing for us to do
since we're there to 'keep the peace'.
Bit of a joke that, Sir,
if you don't mind me saying so.
We were all well and truly
stalled off, Sir, shut up all the time...
Anyhow I think Smithie said I'd cheated,
but I hadn't, Sir,
and he wouldn't leave off
all that night, needling me.
And the next day, on patrol, Sir,
I told him to pack it in
or I'd let him have it...
I didn't mean it, but I was upset...
Then the other two just laughed
and said I was all mouth
and always had been.

It's funny, Sir, I remember really clear
how hot and dusty it was
and I could hear in my head
Sergeant Becker's voice, from combat training,
shouting, shouting,
Kill the bastard! kill,
you little fucking nancy boy...
And I just held my finger on the trigger,
what happened after that was like a dream...'

Non com.

At first, he said, you think of nothing else,
the endless echo and reverberation,
the wicked tick-tock refrain that runs and runs,
what if? what if? what if?
He tells you, hell, it used to keep him
awake nights, he wouldn't want you
to think he was without conscience,
that he hadn't considered...
His soft, grey, young man's eyes try to read
your opinion of him; he twists the key-ring
in his hands as he explains his past.
Not clever enough for college,
no chance to seize the American dream.
He had searched for some way out
of his small town, and the army was glad
of a strong and healthy youth like him.
He got to go to Europe, it was fine,
he got his job to do. It did worry him
at first, but you got used to it, Christ,
they say you can get used to anything in time.
He'd clean forgotten about it till tonight,
but the discussion, the talk, well,
it brought the old fears rushing back...
And say, what do *you* think he should do,
if it finally all came down?
The puzzled boy looks at you with hope,
while you look at him with pity,
and with horror, this small town boy,
not bright enough for college, the last
and smallest link in an obscene chain,
who wonders if, when the order comes,
he could do his job, press
the button, and destroy us all...

Memento mori

Life was always as bright as fever for him,
a snapping comedy of welcome desire.
It pleased him to be pleased,
and that was all he wanted.
The hours of the day were all that mattered.
He had youth, with all its thoughtless courage,
and he was beautiful, because he was so young.
He felt somehow, in some unspoken way,
that he was favoured, privileged, inviolate.
It must be so; how else could it be?
No one he knew had felt the kiss
of tragedy, how else could life be
anything but happiness for him?

When the terrible marks of his affliction
first appeared to him, he chose not to believe.
This happened to others, it couldn't happen
to him, not to him...not to him...
But like a forest fire it crept through him,
unstoppable, his anger could not halt it,
nor his bitterness, and when he asked
for comfort, so many turned away, afraid,
with a fear born of ignorance, blind and cruel.
But those who truly loved him were drawn
still closer, bound to him by a sad, sweet love
that endured the storms.

When it ended, as they had known it would
for so long, he only asked one thing.
That if he had to die, it wouldn't be for nothing,
he wanted the world to learn
from his unlooked-for fate, not just add him
to some list, amend some government statistic,
but by the story of his dying, he might save another
and they use his bright spirit to live,
when he could not...when he could not...

Mary

I always had this idea it was quiet in hospital,
gleaming clean, ice white sheets
glassy from the laundry, folded taut across
the still forms of sleeping patients;
all that stuff of soap opera and myth.
Well, it wasn't like that where I was,
clean and neat, yes, but the noise rose and fell
with the day and night rhythms of illness.
Nurses, tired and always straining against
the long hours of heavy work bustled constantly
up and down the long ward, dragging themselves
through one endless shift to the next.

I wasn't ill at all really, only in overnight
for observation, fine in comparison
with the other women, bulked and shifting
on their rumpled beds.
Out of all of them, you would go by Mary
easily, unnoticing; but as I walked past
she said 'come and talk to me', so I did.
I sat on her bed and looked at her
waxy, pale little face, like an old
Victorian doll, no colour at all,
eyebrows unplucked, brown hair untidily short.
I asked her what was wrong with her,
'I'm an overdose,' she said, with a sort of pride,
as if it were the only interesting thing
she'd ever done.
She'd taken a bottle of pain killers
and set herself to die, aged 21;
but she woke to liver damage, the hospital,
and the shadow of schizophrenia.
Fear moved behind her dark eyes
as she said over and over:

'They want to take me to Lynfield,
I don't have to go, do I?'

I had no answer, the dread of the lunatic asylum
hovered over my head, too, beating
its ragged grey wings in blind panic,
making my mouth dry up and my heart quicken.
I said the things the powerless say
for comfort in the face of terror,
until the gluey-voiced social worker,
with his self-satisfied air of a spare-time priest,
ordered me away.

I sat on my bed and watched
as they tried to persuade her to go quietly.
I could see her stubby fingers clutching her blanket,
I could hear the reedy thread of her voice
protesting under their unctuous murmuring.
The whole ward thrummed with tension;
tears tightened my throat and I prayed
for some miracle of freedom,
her from her fate, and me from my nightmare.
But they wrapped her in her blanket, rolled it
round her like a bandage, so they could say
they don't use straightjackets any more,
and they wheeled her out all trussed up.
As she passed me she flung her head back,
fever-bright eyes burning in her ivory face,
'Goodbye,' she said, in a child's voice,
then she was gone...and I remained.

Whited sepulchres

Dougie sips his tea in the canteen,
sitting alone at the cracked formica table,
his tough, blunt-fingered hands
gripping the mug harder than he thinks.
He is plain and solid looking, his hair
beneath the work cap unfashionably short.
He knows the lads are talking about him,
he can catch the sly glances,
and nearly hear the crude jokes.
He knows what it's all about,
Johnno saw him up the Lane last night,
saw him bartering with Jackie,
and Jackie is a whore...

Now they know he goes with prostitutes.
It was just a rumour before at the works.
The lads are a bit younger than him,
they think it's bloody hilarious,
they think he's a dirty old sod.
Maybe I am, thinks Dougie, sourly,
maybe I am what they say, but at least
I don't pretend, like them. Christ,
they should listen to themselves one day,
going on about how much cash they laid out
on drinks and discos to get some lass
to drop her keks. And Johnno!
He's one to talk an' all!
Last week he did nowt but crack on
about how he got his latest to let him
do it to her without a Durex,
and her not on the pill;
reckoned she deserved it like,
because she carried a pack in her bag,
and 'slags do that'.
God, he's a stupid bastard,
it doesn't feel much different either way,
he just wanted to get one over on her,
show her who was boss...

And there's Kieran, waving those dodgy
gold earrings about, the ones he got off Gaz,
listen to him: 'I'm in tonight, lads!'

They must hate them lasses or be scared of 'em,
they wouldn't go on like that if they weren't.
I don't hate Jackie or Tina,
or the others, it's a fair exchange,
I'm a regular, we know each other,
this is a small enough place,
there's not that many girls, I pay up,
I don't mess 'em about like some,
and we 'ave a little chat sometimes, friendly like.
It's fair, it's honest what we do!
It's not perfect but what in this world is?
And I'd rather have it my way,
God aye, I'd rather have it my way
than theirs...

The forgotten

It wasn't dramatic, no big scenes
or anything like that.
Oh, her Ma did give her a row
about nicking that mascara
but Sandra didn't move out because of that.
No, she just sort of...drifted.
Well, her Dad had long since gone and her Ma...
Ma was a great one for going out.
First off, Sandy stayed at her friend's flat
up Manningham, but it was a bit druggy,
you know, it got on her nerves after a bit.

Eventually, someone said you could
get work easy at the big hotels in Brum,
it was a good laugh, so she packed
her stuff into a holdall and went.
The night before she left
she met her Ma in the Crown.
Sandy told her she was leaving, but Ma was
a bit pissed, didn't seem to take it in,
just got all sloppy, calling her
'my little girl', 'my baby', so Sandy
left home more or less unnoticed.
Took the coach, vanished.

About a year later, her Ma got
engaged again, and seeing Sandy's friend
in a pub, asked her where Sandy had gone.
She wanted her daughter at the wedding
because it was going to be a big, posh do.
The mate said she thought Sand had gone
to London, chambermaiding or summat;
Ma sighed, dabbing at her eye with a tissue.
Oooh, she wouldn't know how to start to look
in a big city like that, oh dear, it's a shame,
but that's that then, i'nt it?
Sandra had gone, the world swallowed her up,
absorbed her; she never came home,
no one noticed, really.

You know, every time there's a big disaster,
when the fire consumes, the train crashes,
the serial killer strikes, or the winter takes
another old person sleeping in a dossbag
on the pavement, have you noticed how
there are always some bodies that are never claimed,
never identified, never asked for?
Did you ever wonder what sort of lives
they lived, solitary and unloved,
those dead people that no one misses,
the ones that no one really noticed
as they just drifted, just
drifted away.

Hobson's choice

I get so tired of it all, that's what it is,
really, I just get so tired of it...
I don't know. It's like, the other day,
right, it was dead sunny, an' I were working
in the salon, with those big glass windows
you can see right out of, you can see everything,
an' all the other lasses were moaning about it
being like a greenhouse an' all the clients
under the dryers were getting dead stalled off;
but all I could think of was, I wish I could go
an' play out, I wish I could get me old
bicycle back, an' go to the shop on it an' get
some chocolate buttons an' some sherbet lemons
an' eat them in the cemetery sitting on the steps
looking out over town, an' not worry
about getting fat, not worry about anything...
Just go an' lie in the long grass that smells
all sort of green and dusty with earth,
an' watch the sparkly bits in the sunshine
float about, then go an' get me tea
an' have Ma give me a hug, an' fall right asleep
as soon as I got in bed an' it be
the school holidays for at least six weeks...
I mean, that's what I thought, honest...

I don't like going home much, now,
'specially since that pig, our Gary, is home
on leave, an' our Mam chasing round after him.
She told me to do his washing last night,
can you credit it? I said let him go do it himsel',
he's done nowt but doss about since he got here,
an' she said he didn't know how to work
the machine, an' I said, what?
He can drive a tank an' kill people,
but he can't work a washing machine?
She was all scratty an' in a real state
like she is these days, giving it,
no lad'll marry you if you go on like that,
an' then she said the exercise'd do me good 'cos

I were getting dead fat; really bitchy, like...
I hated her for that, an' Gary too,
the git, 'cos he had a right laugh.

I want to be a kiddy again...I don't want
to get older, I don't want to be like me Mam...
I mean, I love her an' everything really,
but I don't want to end up like that...
I don't know what I want. Oh, I don't know,
it's just that the sun was shining so nice,
an' I can't stick the smell of perm lotion...
you know...Oh, well, it's no use going on
about it, is it? Come on then,
let's go an' have a cup of coffee, eh?
Here, you don't fancy some Buttons do you?
Go on, we could split a packet,
wouldn't be so fattening that way,
go on, yeah, let's...

Lullaby

When you were little, pyjamas, teddy,
and a nice cup of cocoa,
did your mum leave you a nightlight?
A stumpy, flickering candle in a saucer
that made the curtains dance,
or the landing light left on all night,
because you were scared of the dark,
scared sweaty, dry-mouthed, heart thumping,
paralysed, because of the nameless, shapeless,
hideously formless essence of fear
that changed its scary mask to suit the season;
sometimes a bear, bloody fanged,
or a ghost, revoltingly transparent.
Were you terrified of the boogyman?

Now grown up, sensible, you sleep
in the dark unafraid (except for
those bone-jerking house creaks).
As you lie dozing, do you ever wonder
what happened to the boogyman?
Didn't it grow up, like you?
Didn't it get bigger, more sophisticated,
more...universal? Doesn't it
still make some of us jump and quiver
with the nerve-tingling smack of fear?
Hear it whisper, 'gonna lose your job,
gonna lose the nest egg, lose the car,
lose the stereo, the video, the new clothes,
lose the children...'

All those headlines every day,
all those cheap paper revelations
about the blacks, the homosexuals, the commies,
the beasts who terrorise, subvert, destroy;
all those shrieking column inches
telling us (delicious horror)
of their weird and nasty habits,
their dirty peculiar ideas,
how they lust unceasingly to ruin

our safe and oh so normal lives.
They must be stopped! the greasy pages gibber;
they're everywhere, insidious,
in schools, factories and even on TV.
Everything disturbing is their fault,
the government must act with laws and bills
and clauses to save us, to protect us,
to oppress us all quietly to sleep,
safely in our snug pyjamas, with bars
around our cots and the nightlight on.

And I think it's time we all grew up...

The way it is

Lucy goes to all the gigs, not just
the hometown ones, but all over,
and abroad, sometimes too.
She usually goes by car, sleeping
on the back seat, covered up with coats;
she's often irritable from fatigue
by the time the concert starts.
Still, she gets to meet all the bands.
They usually make a fuss of her,
give her drumsticks, tee-shirts,
that sort of thing.
Not that she hasn't had her fair share
of drunks and druggies stumbling around,
cursing, throwing up and shouting.
Lucy's seen it all, through the thick
blue haze of cigarette smoke.
There's very little she hasn't watched,
deafened by the noise.
Quite the little grown-up, Lucy, aged 6.
Her small face pinched and pale
with tiredness, and the effort of trying
to understand how her mother
wants her to behave tonight;
sometimes she should be still and quiet,
sometimes she should giggle and show off
her dancing, she's often very confused,
but when she gets it right, Mummy,
or Louise as she prefers to be called,
gives her big hugs and kisses,
and everyone laughs.

There's a photograph of me when I was ten,
on holiday with my parents, in Jersey.
I'm perched on a bar stool in the hotel,
legs crossed, holding a pretend cocktail,
little finger crooked, lips pursed,
eyebrows raised in an imitation
of brittle sophistication.

My mother thought that photo was a scream,
I remember posing for it, everyone laughed;
complimented mother on what an amusing child
she had, and I was amusing,
but I was never a child.
Mother never saw why she should alter herself
to accommodate a child, but she liked the way
people paid more attention to her,
admired her, because of me.
I was an excellent accessory, unless I cried.
Lucy's Mother always gets that blank,
cross look too, when Lucy cries.
I recognise it. I can't forget it;
Lucy's worn out, feverish whining
makes me remember the desperation
of being pushed too far, too fast
by that pretty foolish woman.
I know now that that crying
marks the heart forever, locks you up
in some dark internal prison, damaged
and never certain, lonely and frightened
even in the midst of love, because
in their selfishness these women robbed us
of the most precious part of life,
leaving us always looking back
for what we've lost, and seldom seeing
the future we could have.

Dreamtime

In the Dreamtime's solitary walkabout,
the never-never-land,
the child inside, freed from being grown,
summons up the images of might-have-been.
When some shred of conversation
hums half heard in your ear,
when some flickering lie on film
seems to be the truth...then Dreamtime comes,
cat creeping, mist smoking.
Something pains you that you cannot
quite remember, weightless in the past's
dark waters like a drowned swimmer.
A pale face floating, gap-mouthed
under a distortion of the lake;
the soul of fright.

In Dreamtime, the clock spins back
and forth at random, keeping time
for the blind crawling search
for what you've lost and never had.
What's missing; missing some ideal,
some gentle, brave goddess, fierce in anger
and resolutely loyal, some strong
and loving hand to smooth away the fears
and encourage with a word;
the ghost of never-were.
Ask for no consolation,
it isn't there for you to have.
People are so small and careless;
only in Dreamtime, in some pale twilight,
you are safe, safe...In Dreamtime
real mothers can't hurt you any more...

House of dreams

The wind blows cold in your house of dreams,
you want it all to be real,
I'd like to laugh, but my face won't stretch
and you say you want to be healed...
If you turn to me I'll take care of you
but who'll take care of me?

You wander like a saint with a begging bowl
and the daylight hurts your eyes.
I'd like to make you cry, just to see if I could.
Is your heart made of solid steel?
If you turn to me I'll take care of you
but who'll take care of me?

You want everything your hands will cover,
you want more than I can give.
You smile like an angel with eyes full of death,
I can't fight I just surrender.
If you turn to me I'll take care of you
but who'll take care of me?

Maybe you'll kill me, and maybe you won't,
perhaps you'll just drain me dry.
You're a snake in my heart, a flame in my hand
and you'll burn me to the bone.
If you turn to me I'll take care of you
but who'll take care of me?

The wind blows cold in your house of dreams,
you want it all to be real,
I'd like to laugh, but my face won't stretch
and you say you want to be healed...
If you turn to me I'll take care of you
but who'll take care of me?

Bradford (Hometown)

I'd love to say I love it, and sometimes I do
when the sun shines on gold stone
and the rain turns everything to gleaming pewter.
The wind cuts and the streets stink of drains,
it's hometown, after all, some sort of hearthstone.
But when you can't walk out alone
and the hatred, blind and ignorant,
is a trait they breed for;
when resentment and sullen fear
are all too easily read
in eyes deprived of passion
by callous families, rotten schools
and the endless, slow crucifixion
by the society that spawned them.
Oh, when the only battle cry is,
'We're bored, we're dead bored,
make it for us, do it for us,
let us eat your heart and despise you...'
Then I hate it, hate it, hate it
and I wish it was all destroyed,
flattened, finished, ploughed with salt...
Because it isn't good, they aren't nice
and it doesn't fit the dream.
But even though there is no welcome,
no love and no smiling faces,
I still go back, don't I?
We all go back, always, don't we?
To all those towns that scar this sorry island,
we all go back and some of us never leave,
because it's all we've got.

No asylum

When did we become insane?
At what point in our bloody history
did we lose our claim to truth?
What cruel philosophy pointed out to us
the maggot in the meat then made us eat it?
Who told us, whispering wordless implication,
that sex and violence were intertwined,
a woman's lot, a man's right...
Who fed us, mouths agape and waiting,
with the Great Lies, nature's violations,
that women are born wicked and were created
to be slaves, that rape is inevitable
because women provoke it, and all women
can be bought, for all men are buyers?
False logic, constructed to be blinding.

Who severed our sacred partnership, woman and man,
who drove the wedge deep into our hearts
and made us fear each other, who keeps
the vile pot simmering and watches us sicken
from the poison we've all gorged on,
too blind and bribed with promises of Paradise
to see the Great Truth, written in the Earth and Sky?
This society is wrong and it will die.

So we must salvage what we can while we are
still able, love who we can, and be joyful
in that love, reject the Lies and wonder:
When did we become insane?
Oh, when did we become insane?

The visit

Oh yes, I've been to visit her,
it was awful, really,
I've only gone the once, though.
I do feel a bit bad about that,
but really, I couldn't bear it,
it was dead creepy.
I mean, you remember how she was
always laughing and smiling,
not a care in the world you'd have thought,
and ever so brainy, honestly,
the stuff she used to come out with!
The rest of the girls in the office
used to get a bit, well, shocked,
if you like, but sometimes,
if you thought about the things she said,
they did seem right...
but it was all above my head, really.
The others said she was just snobby
always reading books and that
and marrying Chris would settle her down,
like, and force some sense into her.
But she just seemed to get quieter
an' quieter, just drifted round
the office like a ghost.
I got a bit worried about her, actually,
an' asked her what was up,
if she was, well, you know, expecting.
And she said no, and then, well,
I thought she was going to cry,
she looked so strange, and she said,
'He never listens to a word I say, Diane,
ever, no one does...' Well,
I made her a cuppa and told her
to go home for the afternoon...
And it was just after that we heard
she had the breakdown.
Oh, I was upset, of course,
but I weren't really surprised,
if you know what I mean, what with her
being so high-strung and intelligent.

Chris has been fantastic about it all, honest,
he says he won't divorce her, not while
she's in the hospital at any rate.
He confided in me, like, you know,
over a drink last night, told me how
she'd never been a real, proper wife
to him, always going on about daft stuff
and forgetting the housework,
but he wanted to do the decent thing by her.
He's a fantastic guy, you know.
Anyhow, I told him about what happened
when I went to see her in that hospital,
her all tatty and vacant seeming
in a grotty old dress and slippers,
twisting at her wedding-ring
and not saying a word until I got up
to go, and then she said,
'Diane, don't get wed, it's a thing
lads thought up, to get themselves
a slave and an unpaid prostitute, it is.'
Well! I mean! Just imagine!
What an awful thing to say!
But I thought, well, you can tell
she's not right in the head, poor thing,
coming out with stuff like that...
But I couldn't go back again,
you understand, don't you?
It was too creepy for words,
but it must be, like, really awful
to be mad, and I do feel ever so sorry
for her, oh yeah, that I do.

The promise

Maybe my memory is faulty;
I do recall I made some vow or other,
wasn't there some promise
to do this or that; or, I think,
not to do something, yes,
not to put myself through this again.
But still the wheel turns
and I am bound upon it.
Oh, I'll just have a drink,
smoke a cigarette, eat some chocolate,
watch TV without seeing what I watch,
I won't pick up the phone.
I won't write the letter.
I won't go to where he'll be,
oh, I won't do a lot of things,
or wonder if he thinks of me,
or if he's simply glad to get away
without a scratch.
Despite what foolish songs
and foolish singers say,
there is no romance in this little death at all.
But if, as my good friend assures me,
there are a million people in the world
feeling just the way that I do now,
then I'll raise my glass and drink to them,
and think, perhaps, that one of them
is doing the same, somewhere, for me...

Pamela

I went to school with this girl called Pamela,
I didn't like her very much, she wasn't my type.
She had a horrible haircut
and wore thick make-up all the time;
she didn't like the same sort of music as me
and she always wore a black bra
under her white school blouse.
She wasn't in our clique, her major cronies were
Pat, the ugly girl, and Anne, the class victim.
You could always hear them breathing, 'Oh, Pammy,
you never, what did he do then? Honestly, really?'
We all used to go to the same disco
on Fridays, though, it was a small town
and there was nowhere else to go.
Pamela was always in a clinch
with some unsavoury youth in a dark corner,
while we did the latest dances
and sneered at the skinheads from Bilton estate
behind their backs...Eventually,
Pamela started to go steady with one of her boys,
we didn't know him, he was a bit older than us
and had a job at a garage in town.
Pammy was seen to be wearing his chrome ID bracelet
which meant they were as good as engaged,
or it did when we were 15.
Soon it was all over school that they'd done it,
Pamela walked about with a knowing smirk
and the toilets were rife with speculation.
Then it was the summer holidays, but when we got back,
Pamela just wasn't around, not in school,
not at the dance, not in the café, not anywhere...
At first we didn't miss her, we never
hung round with her after all, then one day
Pat burst into hysterics in class
for no apparent reason, and had to be
taken home by a teacher in a car.
Well, we were dumbstruck, so we got Anne
at break, and forced it out of her;
of course it was all about Pamela.

What had happened was this: she had got pregnant
by her boyfriend, they used to do it in the park
on Friday nights after the disco, of course
they didn't mention contraception, I suppose
he assumed she was on the pill and she would
never have asked him to use a condom,
if she even knew what they were.
She told him about the baby in the pub
they used to go to, he said OK, don't worry,
then he said he was going to the Gents,
but he didn't come back. After a while
Pamela went to look for him at his house,
but when she rang the bell, his mother answered,
screaming at her, saying she was a whore,
a slag, a little bitch, and she needn't think
her Geoff was going to marry the likes of Pamela
so she could just bugger off out of it.
Pamela cried and begged to see Geoff
but he just hid while his mother slammed the door
so Pamela trailed home alone, sobbing.
She knew she couldn't tell her parents,
it was impossible, unthinkable,
totally out of the question.
She sat up awake in her pink bedroom all night,
then, first thing, she packed a duffle bag,
went to the bank, got out her savings
and caught the coach to London, though
what she thought she'd do there, god knows,
she'd never been before, she knew no one,
but I suppose we all thought London
was the answer to everything, somehow.
Well, she wandered about all evening, worn out,
terrified and lost, until she found herself in a park.
That made her cry again, thinking of Geoff and how
she loved him despite what he'd done.
She sat on a bench, tears pouring down
her face, and she knew that there was
nothing else for her to do. So,
taking a knitting-needle out of her bag
she pulled her knickers down and stuck it
hard up inside herself, once, twice,
until she fainted.

36

A young policeman found her, he picked her up
and ran with her to the road.
He held her in his arms while the thick blood
pumped out of her, soaking his uniform
down to his boots.
They got her to hospital just in time,
she didn't die, but of course she'd never
be able to have children or anything.
Her family moved out of town
shortly afterwards, went down south.
We never saw Pamela again; it was all
a long time ago in the 70s.
Things were different then.
Probably nowadays she could have
an abortion in the hospital,
clean and safe...probably...

The rain

Imagine you're in a café in town,
in the Mona Lisa, having a cup of tea,
Michael Jackson on the juke-box.
You're waiting for your food to arrive,
staring out of the plate-glass window.
It's coming dark early these days
it's raining hard now
blurring the shop lights across the road
and the car headlights passing by.
Then suddenly, for a moment,
someone is staring back at you,
standing in the pouring rain
almost lost in the silver-threaded dusk.
A creature without substance,
the sharp rain seeming to slide
through the pale flesh of its face,
indistinct and ghostly faded,
hair slapped down to its head
by the streaming water.
It is motionless, only wavering
because of the sleety distortion.
You lock together for a second,
its dark eyes a deep but smoky glaze,
the person hangs like a stain
in the splashing twilight
and then they're gone;
suddenly you realise the record's changed
but you hadn't noticed,
you peer out of the rain-beaded glass
at nothing, at a wet street.
The girl brings your food and you eat,
without really tasting, wondering.

I saw you in that café window,
haloed in the golden light
like an angel in a medieval manuscript.
Your eyes stopped me
in my aimless wandering
like a hook; and I stared back,

hunching myself up against
the icy slivers of water,
cold hands bony and fisted in my pockets.
I felt like a shadow rolling inside
a hollow shape of human flesh,
a camera looking out from the sockets
where my eyes should be...
I was frozen for that moment
repelled but unable to resist,
as your life unrolled for the filming,
all that you were, will be, are now
unravelled for me
in the exchange of our glance,
filling me with unwanted knowledge
like so many times before.
I felt that the rain pounding on my skull
would wash me away, a spirit already,
unbound to earth, unhuman.
You were hot and thoughtless,
glowing, veined and bursting
with life and blood, alive...

I envy you,
I always have,
now do you understand?

Rosie

When I got home after that long
cold bus ride, I made some strong tea
and ran a hot bath, remembering
how that used to be our cure-all.
I thought about those lunch hours
we spent laughing in the Ladies
and painting each other's faces,
stopping in watching television
with the sound off and doing
the dialogue ourselves, drinking cider
and making weird clothes
with my grandmother's sewing-machine.
Braiding up our hair
and crying after the disco
and some lad's thoughtless cruelty...
There was nothing that couldn't be
made better with cups of black tea
and telling the tale over and over
until the pain went out of it.
On holiday that time, jeans rolled up
and feet blue with cold,
we ran away from the waves
and ate ice cream sundaes,
to hell with the diets and who
is that pretty boy?

You were my best mate, Rosie,
the last best mate of my youth,
but you got engaged to Mike,
gold chains, nice suits, wine bars,
and when I called for you that day,
oh, Rosie, you wouldn't let me
in the house, just made me stand
in the drive while you told me
Mike didn't want you
to hang around with me any more,
because I was a bad influence,
and you shut the door in my face.

I was glad it was raining
because you couldn't see me crying;
you know, when friends split up,
it hurts for the longest time.
It must have been fifteen years ago
but it still catches in my heart,
Rosie, and twists
like the Judas kiss.

Tattoo two

When I was a small child I lived by the sea,
not amongst the tattered glittering façades
of some resort, but the grey and basic
working world of the naval port;
the fairground and the prom tacked on
loosely, an afterthought.
On Sundays, sometimes, we would walk
into the teeth of the wind, crunching
along the pebble beach to the beacon
of the big wheel, rolling in the sky above
the fair, candy floss and shooting galleries;
the Waltzer, the Whip, and the whole place
full of sailors.

There were always hollow-eyed matelots lolling
exhaustedly around the brilliant lure
of the old-fashioned tattoo booths,
their boarded fronts painted with writhing
fleshy pink mermaids, emerald fish-tails thrashing,
jostling the disdainful peacocks, bold eyes
staring from their feathers, and the obligatory dragons,
their bulging corkscrew bodies a riot
of violent-coloured scales and crests
that owe nothing to the orient.
On boys' arms, hula girls, boss-eyed
and top heavy, danced on skinny biceps,
or black panthers dug their claws in,
and suffering Jesus was crucified
over and over on scrawny chests concave
with their passion for decoration.

Although I was dragged away
by scandalised parents, the seed
was planted, and it grew...
So when, years later, I went
to the tattooist in my turn, put
my trust in the artist's steady hands,
I felt no panic when the blood came,
mixed with black, I didn't mind the pain

and I felt none of the regret
the untattooed harp on about so hopefully.
I feel none now, only a little sad and tired,
that those who can't create themselves
can desire with such fear and violence
to ridicule and destroy what they will not even
try to understand. There is
no terrible mystery, there are no dark secrets,
no weird, perverted motives,
no rebel without a cause clichés,
just the pleasure of creation
and the adrenalin of commitment.

Treasure in the heart

I should have got up and shouted,
I should have said something,
I should have had the courage
in that sickly, stupid, hideous place;
they called it a 'chapel',
full of formica pews and fabric flowers
and only ten of us there to mourn,
washed by the treacly thread of taped organ music
tricking fatuously in the background,
while this fat, untidy, Christian woman
rolls out sonorously the imbecile clichés
about my grandmother, who she never saw
even in death, but I saw her,
my grandmother,
her terrible strength and sword-sharp truthfulness,
the unforgivable power of the strong woman,
lying shell-thin and faded silvery
in that horrible, neat and tidy, rest home room.
I heard that breathing, rattling and moaning
as she drifted through sleep to her solitary dying,
and it was me who cried and spoke,
words falling hollow into the still space,
words about guilt, and love, and missed opportunities
and love, and love...
Me, snotty nosed and sticky-faced with tears,
not grown up at all, no, still a child
searching for forgiveness and for family,
regretting stupid neglect,
never to know if she heard,
or if she even knew I was there.
Oh, my grandmother, oh, my Nana,
nine minutes that stupid ceremony took,
nine minutes, I timed it
by the plastic clock on the wall,
and I didn't have the nerve to say,

'Listen to me! She was fierce and proud,
brave, wicked and possessive!
All the things she had to be,
and she deserved more than this,
we all deserve more than this, in the end...'

But I said nothing,
and I'm sorry Nana, I'm really sorry.

Nemesis

There's an estate at the back of our house,
a sprawl of ill-built council houses,
pebble-dash peeling and broken fences.
One of the families has a mongrel puppy
that keeps running lost into our garden,
so I take it back to them, often.
The woman always answers the door,
standing blinking, framed
by the greasy darkness of the hallway,
a tumble of grubby children clutching
at her skirt: I hold the puppy,
she stares at me, mouth slightly open.
I hand the wriggling, licky dog to her,
and like a worn-out cassette
excuses whine from her,
the same ones she uses to everyone, always.
'It's not my fault, couldn't help it, like,
I 'ad him tied up, kids did it...'
Once her husband was there,
short, stocky, red-faced, reckoned himself
cock of the street, beer gut straining
his shirt buttons.
I got a real mouthful off him,
she just stood there staring
like a broken doll, while the kids
set to howling...

While he was yelling at me,
I noticed one of the kids, the eldest,
wasn't crying with the rest.
I must have been staring,
because the child looked up at me,
and in his snotty, grimy face
eyes bright with intelligence shone at me:
I can't forget that, I can't forget
the stab of surprise and the horrible knowledge
of what that bright child's life will be:
with his worn-out zombie mother,
and his stupid drunken father,

cheated of his chances in useless schools,
ignored by corrupt and wicked government,
denied, beaten, dispossessed and shoved
into the numbing inevitable round
of frustration, fighting and savage boredom,
while the children of the middle classes
piss away their privilege
in the Student Union bars,
and prop up the tottering society
that shelters their inadequacies.

Everything faded but the child's gaze
as he stood at the rickety gate,
his fate certain and damned.
And I want to pull all this injustice down,
destroy it all in blood and fire,
not next year, not tomorrow,
but now, this moment, this very second,
level it, raze it and start again clean,
so he's got a hope, so we've all got a hope...

The quality of mercy

Sunlight slanted down from a high narrow window,
across the courtroom, specks of dust
glowing brightly, drawn up into its gold.
I remember fixing my eyes on that familiar illumination,
as I did when I was a child, to try to still my nerves.
My whole body shook, teeth chattered, stomach rolled.
Icy steel wires tunnelled through my flesh, vibrating.
To control my hands, I drew on the sheet of paper
in front of me, while solicitors and barristers
went through their paces.

I listened, shivering again, this time with fury,
as the pink-cheeked young policeman
recited his evidence, like a dim schoolboy
speaking a poem learned by heart for homework.
Over this room, thick with the smell
of humanity, of fear, sweat and sorrow,
hunched the magistrate, impatient and shallow,
immune to the sour, creeping odour
of unnecessary lies, petty corruption
and little, everyday evils,
one tenth of the wicked iceberg visible
as the rest bulked sinister
in the dank waters rolling around us.

Taking my turn in the box,
the greasy wooden rail under my hands,
the fear left me so all I could think of
was how very, very stupid and petty
this all was, the police and the courts,
the blind leading the blind, the corrupt
dancing with the hypocrite,
all that our country has become displayed
in this sham, this sick and sorry comedy...

Drawn up tight as fever, I gave the useless answers
and was marked down on their ledgers,
guilty as charged. Later, in another court,
another judge cleared my name

because people raised the money to buy me some justice.
And what makes me angry, what makes my fists clench
and my heart pound, is that if the police
would lie in such an unimportant case,
cynically, casually and as a matter of course,
what ragged, tottering towers of deception
do they construct to get a quick result
on a serious case, polish up their image
and satisfy a hungry media lost to honour
howling out for monsters, villains, devils and demons.
We all know what they do; with horrible regularity
they jail the unlucky, the poor, the misfit, the innocents,
they jail some for reasons even more vile and dangerous,
sitting targets, easy prey, they jail them
for simply being black, or being Irish...

The list

Who adds them to the list
all those who die at the torturer's hand?
What mark is left to signal that they lived?
How many millions pass unknown
grieved for only by their families,
the voices of their loved ones raised
then silenced, by the leaden pressure of fear.
What is there to comfort them
as they cower in the few hours respite
from the electric shock, the knives,
the beatings and the vileness,
crouched in darkness on some slimy concrete floor,
patterned with burns from the cigarettes
their captors stubbed out on them with a sneer.
What crime did they commit to warrant this?
Just a careless word, an opinion voiced,
and then a friend's betrayal.
Ah, do they forgive that betrayal
now they understand why it happened,
and who will they betray unwilling in their agony?
So, who marks their passing then,
the screaming victims and silent dead,
who adds them to the list?

When you raise your voice to argue in the pub,
when they print your letter of protest
in the local paper,
remember them, mark them,
the shadows of the tortured
who die in filth and horror,
for what we think are our rights.

The wait

The night falls humid, sultry, velvet dark.
The air is thick as cream and hardly moved
by the slow, faint breeze that breathes
on the curtain of dull emerald creeper
masking the high brick garden wall.
I wait again for my body to tire
as my mind, fretful and restless, will not.
I only want to sleep, to slide
into dreams like water, warm and undemanding,
I want the hours to pass without my knowing it,
and the gold gauze of morning be here quickly
so this house, like a prison self-chosen,
comfortable, and so unleavable, will have no more
hushed corners of darkness secret and dusty
with old wormy thoughts and dim obsessions.

I want to lie quietly in crumpled pale sheets
that still retain the faint, sweet smell of you
and relive memories, rearrange memories
like photographs laid out in playing-card formations:
the colour of your eyes, bitter chocolate,
the slightly bruised shadows, mauve
as the bloom on ripened plums, that lie
beneath the gleaming glaze of your skin,
the skull so visible beneath the thin flesh,
moulding only closer with the years.
I want to remember words of love and anger,
I want to feel some point of contact.
I hate this waiting, and it seems to me
you pace your days away
in some enemy camp, distant and cold,
and more than barbed wire and bars keeps us apart;
the shallow days so slow in passing.
This night falls silently in veils of stars.
I would sleep if you were here, but you are not,
and so the Earth turns as I lie waking,
and if I could spin my spirit from my body
and fetch you home again unscathed,
I would, I would.

Ambition

The wheel turns and we spin with it,
no help for us who've made our path.
We see our fate and never try to fight it,
because it calls us even as it kills.
There is no pain like separation
but we embrace it as we should each other,
the parting kiss and say goodbye,
the long wait grinds like a broken bone.

Through the night's pale consolations,
a drink too many and a pretty face,
I only see your sad eyes shining,
the light of a star on a frosty night.
Oh, the words come thick and stumbling,
stupid, clumsy clichés, all used up.
All those phrases speak so slick and easy,
They roll like thunder and beat hollow
like an empty drum.

It's not enough, it's not enough,
too many questions that we dare not answer
and the truth is only something
that we sing for strangers, far away.
And yes, we're tired, yes, we're lonely
and as the days crawl by distracted,
the grand design seems sham and aimless,
but we still play the game because we made it
and wait for the return as best we can.

In memoriam

Our mothers' mothers, our grandfathers'
grandfathers, they were the link,
they spoke in the voice of the storm,
their power was the everlasting breaking
of the waves, the bright days' repetition
and the seasons' rolling wheel.
They showed us the endless chain
of what we were, our mothers' mothers,
our grandfathers' grandfathers, back and back
they went, every name remembered.
The voices of their wisdom, all that they had learned
was not lost to us, we were not alone,
stranded under the pitiless skies.
We had the bloodlines of the clans,
our children were not tiresome strangers to us
but the link that forged the future.

The shamans, trance-bound in holy ecstasy,
taught us all that the past contained,
we were part of LIFE, we had pride,
dignity and reason. Now all we are
are scuttling beasts savage in our isolation,
worthless in our own eyes, severed
from out common memories, without
the knowledge of our history...

Oh, of all the wicked things you did to us,
listen, Christian, close to me,
of all the violence done
in your messiah's name,
the worst and the most subtle was
you robbed us of our ancestors,
you cut the path behind us
and you took away our names.

Requiem

Slowly, slowly, the heavy golden days
slide past like honey off a spoon.
The fire hisses and the wind outside
shakes the windows in their frames.
People pass outside, their lives like tramlines,
moving in some silent, ritual passage,
faces blank as water, their eyes folded and secret,
clutching themselves to themselves
corsetted and strapped against the world's tricks...
Nothing makes them jump.

These autumn weeks slip past
like a timeless river, never to return,
a sightless melancholy washes the faces, and the streets;
they say that those who die from exposure
at the end, cuddle in their snow shrouds
as if it were a lover's arms,
warm and sleepy as the Lady takes them home
for the last time;
as the storm clouds of hysteria thicken and rumble
on horizons far away,
I wonder if this stupor is our last golden dream
and if we'll ever wake from it again.

Legend

And over all the land is a shadow,
breathing and alive, but still invisible;
a tainted cloud, the lord of the flies.
A silent, drifting miasma
that coils and creeps into every soul,
then alters and spoils.
It shows in little ways,
in meanness and in petty spite,
in ignorance and cruelty.
A beaten child, a ruined river,
desertion and betrayal;
every heart a potential Judas,
every soul willing to sell cheap.
The land is overlaid with discontent...

And yet, somehow, we still believe
a hero will come, a shining one,
and deliver us from this biting evil.
That Arthur and his Companions
still sleep, unwaking, waiting
for the clarion call to save us,
that in our last hour of need
we'll all be swept away and rescued
by some fabled Jesus and a last judgement.
And in this faith unspoken,
unmentioned, a sort of hope,
we wait, and wait, and wait, and wait,
all unknowing, that the only heroes
are us.

Red Sky

And the sun rises; every day the promise renewed,
red and gold in clouds and fire,
a torch to light the world,
a burning brand that sheds its brilliance
on all those questions that we'd rather not recall.
Freed of the night's formless worrying,
sleepless, twisting uncomfortably
in our sour beds, the daylight, cooled
and innocent illuminates our plight.

Tell me, do you take your anger and let it
ash into apathy? Will our time upon
the living body of the Earth be remembered
only for what we didn't do,
didn't say, didn't make?
That fury, that we douse with excuses
and petty fears, could, fashioned
into a living weapon, be our salvation.
The questions flood the waking mind
with formless apprehension,
will our young men just destroy themselves
in slops and bitterness? They who should be
our bulwark against the lies of the State.
Will our young women, Nature's forged warriors
persistent and true, grovel in the bondage
of wilful ignorance, self-made slavery and greed?
We could make something of ourselves...
have some posterity. There is so much to save,
yet we feel dwarfed and useless in the shadow
of corruption, vast, cruel and unjust.
But as the light fades and the night returns,
if we look outside, outside of our unease
and discomfort, we can see the reasons
for the battles waiting to be fought:
the moon shows in a silver web
a weird and magic landscape, hypnotic,
even in the shattered glitter of a city streetlamp.

All this beauty: all the rage and power
of the storm, the heart's ease
calm of still water gleaming
in the hollow crown of the brindled hills,
all the glory of the Earth is ours
and in trust for our children.
Should we allow it to be destroyed
by the wormy self-interest of leaders
not fit to lead, their lives controlled
by avarice and the dictates of dishonour?
While the sun rises, every day,
every day is another chance
to laugh at death and fight...
Not a chance to change the world,
just to change the filth that runs it
and make a clean sunrise.

Circus Circus

Well, of course, it's the circus pulling into town, everyone piling off the tour buses still asleep, still cramped from a night rolling around in a coffin-sized bunk (how we laugh at all the press revelations about sex-in-a-bunk Scandinavian superstars and their kiss and tell groupies doing it like frenzy all over *their* bus. God knows you can't even have a wank in one of those coffins without the whole bus knows. Mind, perhaps huge fame brings huge bunks)...wearing weirder and weirder clothes as the tour goes on and the reality slips away. We're the raggle-taggle gypsies oh, the outlaws, the travellers and all that romance. That's how some people see it; not us, really, not any more. I feel it sometimes, that apartness, that glamour, but that's not surprising.

So, anyhow, today we pull in to some place or another, some large ex-industrial wasteland city, and while performers and friends and relatives of performers and merchandisers and managers of performers snore the morning away, the crew crawl up and start to build a place for the group to do what they're paid to do. They creep about scaffolding and do intricate things with wire and gaffer tape, they make the magic circus work, the pretty coloured lights and the big noise. We sleep – they work, that's the way it is. They're probably glad we're not there stumbling about getting in the way, tripping over multicore and attempting to engage them in conversation. We have our work, they have theirs, and they wouldn't walk on stage in the middle of a show and try to bum a fag off of the singer, but we do that to them all the time. They're quite tolerant really, and treat us like toddlers at the 'but why?' age.

This so-called nightclub is a ghastly sight in the grey light of day that's struggling down through the get-in door. I imagine it's supposed to be glossy, sophisticated and relentlessly chrome, but that's at night when it's usually full of young people paying a deal of money to have fun, when the disco is loud and the lights round the bar are pink. The club next-door, which you can get into from this place, is done up as a surrealist's nightmare of Easter Island, complete with replica Easter Island heads. Some people should never take drugs, especially not club designers. Still, whoever did that one obviously got took away and this club is the usual Meccaette dross.

We don't fit in here. Not the crew, not the performers, not the friends of, or the fans of, not even the managers of. It stinks of old alcohol and cigarettes, and the pinky-grey carpet is slick with dirt. I screw up my eyes in the afternoon gloom and gather my robes about me for warmth. It's cold as a B.R. waiting room in here and the pungent odour of damp tickles my nose. No showers in this dump, I recall wistfully, and the dressing rooms...well, I wouldn't house a whippet in those conditions.

I look for a friend. There are none. I look for someone to ponce a fag off, thus introducing the possibility of human contact. I scan the area. Besides the crew who are ignoring everyone except each other, and the merchandiser attempting to put up his stall in the opposite corner against horrendous odds, spontaneously collapsing tables and a colossal hangover, there is only the Following in.

The Following – that motley selection of individuals that come to every gig the performers do. We know them, they know us, and our relationship is at once intimate and alien. We know they know our work in a strange way better than we do, and certainly in a way we never will, and we have conversations, but the gulf is unbridgable, even if they wanted us to bridge it, which I strongly suspect they don't. They are a tribe. They belong to each other, and like any tribe they tear each other to bits at every opportunity. They snitch and bitch and bad mouth each other, and come together in one glorious display of unity only when in the presence of outsiders. And like a family robbed of its parents, a band of orphans, they patch each other up and herd each other from town to town with impressive accuracy and passion. They sit there, on the greasy velour banquettes in a litter of doss bags and nylon holdalls, sending out scouts to find unused power points to plug their crimping irons into, for their brief hours of finery before fatigue and sweat destroys the afternoon's creativity. They are here for us, but completely of themselves. They eye me warily, pretending not to look, but I am well practised and catch the sliding eye. I pass the time of day with a couple of them I know, they supply a cigarette and reply to my comments with the air of tribal people conversing with someone touched by the finger of God, or if you like – mad.

It's all just a way of passing time. We are all waiting for the show tonight. The crew, the band, the Following, me, we all wait, and like people waiting at a railway station for a delayed train, we make desultory conversation.

Eventually the group soundcheck, boringly, because there's no interesting way to do it, and while it should just be a technical operation to test equipment and discover the awfulness of the acoustics, they are not unaware that there are a sort of pre-audience in there listening, so they semi-perform, playing covers and chaffing each other. Sometimes it's more interesting than the gig because they are still themselves – nice ordinary men. They haven't yet become transformed by nerves and adrenalin into strangers; sweating fighters. The crew take great pains to look technical and efficient, and they can't erase a certain smugness as the check progresses, and they're seen to solve, with devastating efficiency and yards of gaffer tape, certain apparently fatal flaws in the venue. To an extent this is their performance, and they play to the gallery...but cool.

When all this travail is over, rather than face the dressing-room, the group drive off to a local radio interview, usually done by a slick DJ who would prefer to be working for daytime Radio One – and shows it. He gets the lads' names wrong and has never heard their records. He doesn't feel this matters, and he doesn't think the listeners notice that he is an ill-informed prat; he is wrong, of course, but that is not something he would ever consider. In his studio, he prefers to be God. The only item that impresses him is that the group once appeared on Top of the Pops. This does not impress the group who hated every naff and cringy moment of it, and wouldn't mind telling the world that given a quarter of chance. The DJ however, does not care to have his icons mocked. He has a conversation with himself, and the group, who are conscientious, try to talk to the people who are listening. Soon the whole thing grinds to a halt and the lads escape to an Italian restaurant; to eat their disappointment away; all except the lead singer who can't eat after midday on show days because he is nervy and temperamental and has a bad throat. He nibbles a piece of garlic bread and dreams of motorway breakfast at 4.30 in the morning.

Back at the venue, the Ladies is rancid with the stink of burning lacquered hair, and the lasses sit about on the pink paisley carpet painting their faces and drinking cheap wine. The scandals and gossip of the previous night are picked over at length and the boys of the Following are derided for their lack of appreciation and general uselessness. The odour of old Patchouli permeates the air and the calling is only interrupted when one girl who is pregnant expresses a serious lust for fresh tomatoes. A Ninja raid on a nearby grocer's is planned. We still wait...

Out in the hall, or disco as you please, the merchandiser is attempting to tot up last night's takings and stock-take before the punters are let in. An expression of puzzlement deepening into desperation creases his usually devil-may-care features; will he get it all together in time? Will the posters he has gaffer-taped to the flock wallpaper hold up all night in what will shortly be a sauna? Will the trestle tables collapse under the weight of eager buyers? *He* collapses in a rainbow heap amongst a pile of unboxed tee-shirts and has a fag...life's hard for a hippy with a capitalist conscience. Today psychedelia, tomorrow C&A.

The management of the club are twittering about the place moaning about everyone wearing clogs, Yorkshire clogs that is, none of your effete backless Scandinavian rubbish. The management seem curiously blind to the damage already perpetrated on their dancefloor by the hordes of stiletto-heeled madams thrashing the previous nights away to lady Madonna.

The bouncers flex their muscles and try to terrify the merchandiser into giving them free tee-shirts. He laughs gaily at them with the air of a man pushed to the limit of his endurance. The bouncers are worried by his insouciance, and wander off with furrowed brows. They take their puzzlement out on several fifteen-year-olds who have bought tickets at HMV and now aren't being allowed in because they're under-age. The venue didn't see fit to mention on the publicity that it was over 18s only, neither do they wish to give refunds. The children grieve and plaint outside and the bouncers growl and wodge about until the overworked, underpaid and unappreciated tour manager sorts out what he can with the blind energy of a Jack Russell after a rabbit. Everyone hates the tour manager because he is too harassed to massage everyone's egos, and he threw tact to the winds years ago, if indeed he ever knew what it meant. He is the Juggernaut of the organisation and this is his finest hour.

The Following meanwhile have mastered the intricacies of the guest list system which allows them varying numbers of places after the friends and relatives of band and crew. The Following are thereby obliged to be responsible for themselves; to decide for themselves and rotate their names on the list every night. To a generation terrified of not being liked and petrified of responsibility, this is indeed a crushing blow. The person delegated by default to pick the favoured few was a person apart, shunned and vilified by their erstwhile comrades, a tragic figure of heartache and persecution...at least he was until the lasses took it over and just got on with it. Still, the accusations, snobbery, egomania and injured pride were terrible to behold; I'm sure Hitler wasn't hated as much as the poor sucker who had to deliver the dreadful news of their exclusion to those who were rotated out that night. The unfortunates who then stand about outside the venue poncing 10p off all and sundry are collectively known as The Glums. They take their defeat very, very badly.

Tonight the rumour abounds that a music press journalist is going to grace our little gathering. This cheery news serves to take the Following's mind off its guest listitis and many and colourful are the fates planned for the representative of those august journals of music should anyone see through his/her disguise and find them out. The general consensus is that tar and feathering would be a let-off. The hacks of the music rags are held in about the same esteem as a rabid sewer rat – but with considerably less brain. The band dislike them, the crew couldn't care less if they lived or died, but on the whole, death would be preferable. We wait like panting hyenas to see if we can spot the difference between the journalist and a normal punter.

Then the doors open and the venue floods with people. The merchandiser is hit by a wave of consumers wishing to be in the swim by wearing a band name tee-shirt during the gig. We think they'd be better off saving it so they could change into something dry after, but different strokes…The tee-shirt stall trestle-tables are being squeezed into the hall by the pressure of bags, coats and sweaters that are shoved underneath them like cast off Christmas puppies. The merchandiser futilely mutters about not taking responsibility but no one heeds him and the Everest of leathers grows. Lots of them are painted on the back with the group's latest record cover, or previous record covers, and we judge these critically. Most are adequate, some are excellent but it's the really duff ones that are dear to our hearts, especially the one that's so distorted the faces of the group they look even more simian than the NME would have us believe.

Soon the hall is packed with a bewildering array of cultists, ranging from ex-soul boys to bikers and every sort of gothpunk and semi-psychedelic in between. All have one thing in common, they can't afford the bar prices. After what seems like several hours of the sound engineer's choice of tapes, presumably some sort of bizarre revenge trip, the support band play. This is always a worrying time as they are usually so patently nervous (unless of course they're Scandinavian) that wondering if they'll survive to the end of their alloted span without psychic crisis takes most of your concentration. The Following are kindly and applaud vigorously, but the locals eye the musicians with an indifference bordering on contempt. It's very hard indeed being a support so we're sympathetic and think Strengthening Thoughts at the stage.

Soon all is clear again and the sound man has another burst of taped insanity. We are getting very blasé about his musical idiocy but startled expressions pass over the faces of some of the punters when Wigan's Ovation strike up 'Skiing in the Snow'. The stage is a mass of crew and the tour manager has a poised quality about him which means a lot if you've known him for a while. The average Joes just think he's glassy-eyed from drink. The intro tape goes on. Conversations stop in mid-word. People hand me their spectacles and the boys strip to the waist. Some of us are glad they go no further and deplore the craze for running shorts. The area in front of the stage is a heaving mass of punters. A few preliminary chants begin. The intro seems to go on forever, and the atmosphere is heavy with anticipation. I sit on the collapsible tee-shirt stall and cadge a smoke. I wait for the opening chord and watch the ecstatic surge of humanity when the group stride on like gladiators.

Gone, gone, gone are the nervous affable men of the afternoon. Now an arrogant wiry savage stalks around the front of the stage and the unfinished, disconnected tunes of the soundcheck are blasted into powerful anthems. The gleaming warriors on their platform step neatly and with a certain visable joy through the exhibition of their creativity. This is what they love doing and they do it very well, this is the trance of passion the crowd have come to experience. Here is the reality of those songs they have played over and over in their bedrooms...here is the living proof of their belief. The Following trip steadily through their routines, each song with its own particular mime and movement. They stand in circles to complete their mysteries and their cool is unity and perfection. The boys, of course, spar like demons, reasonably painless on the whole, just the occasional bloody nose or split lip. They aren't vicious, but they are, shall we say, physical...The group spin an adrenalin magic irresistible in its glorious disregard for appearances or reserve, they both transport and are transported by the accuracy of their performance and they drive the crew demented trying to resuscitate used-up guitars.

The spider's web of glittering lights blinds and dazzles and the sound gets louder and piercingly clear...then it's all over. The encores taken, guitars rescued, the house-lights are on and the band sit shattered and soaking in the dank glory of the dressing-rooms drinking beer and cheap wine, anything to make up the fluid lost in sweat, and they slump with wet towels round their necks like three boxers after a needle match.

Out in the venue, the tee-shirt king has disappeared with his assistants under a writhing mass of soggy, happy people all wanting several variations of the same thing; a tee-shirt, two posters and three badges, two tee-shirts, four posters and one badge, two badges and can I have my bag please it's the one underneath everything at the back. The crew are shifting boxing up and shoving equipment around with alarming rapidity and the bouncers are in their element bullying any small, thin children they can get hold of. Soon even the Following have gone and the only outsiders left are a small, dedicated group from a fanzine who are attempting to interview an exhausted lead singer, and several giggly young women who want their photos taken with the drummer. Eventually even they drift off, the crew load out, the merchandiser flutters away in his jester's motley and the band limp onto the tour bus. Immediately an argument ensues between the tour manager and the lead singer about stopping for a motorway breakfast on the way to the next town. Singer wins by pulling rank and the crew watch Spinal Tap on video and get drunk. After breakfast all fall, stagger or squeeze themselves into their bunks and snore daintily as the bus driver weaves gently across England to the next town.

It's the magic circus...it's the gipsy jokers...it's a gig, like a million others, and like nothing else that's ever been. It's what we are.